Finding Your Authentic Self

An illustrated journey to well-being

Written and illustrated by
Jessica Fan

AWAKING OCTOPUS PRESS

Copyright © 2023 by Jessica Fan

All rights reserved. No part of this book may be reproduced or used in any manner without written permission of the copyright owner except for the use of brief quotations in a book review.

First hardcover edition 2023

Book design by Jessica Fan

ISBN 9781738874507 (hardcover)
ISBN 9781738874521 (paperback)
ISBN 9781738874514 (e-book)

www.jessicafan.ca

For the gentle, loving voice within each of us.

We are each born into this world
radiant, beautiful, and *whole.*

Our Authentic Self shines from within,
nourished by a deep source of life energy.

As we grow, we are taught that there are "right" ways of being and "wrong" ways of being.

We may learn that it is not safe
to express our Authentic Self.

We may start to believe
that it has no worth.

Out of fear and shame,
we create armour to protect us.

Some of us build emotional walls
that hide us from the world.

Some of us pursue
perfection, fame, and fortune,
hoping to validate our existence.

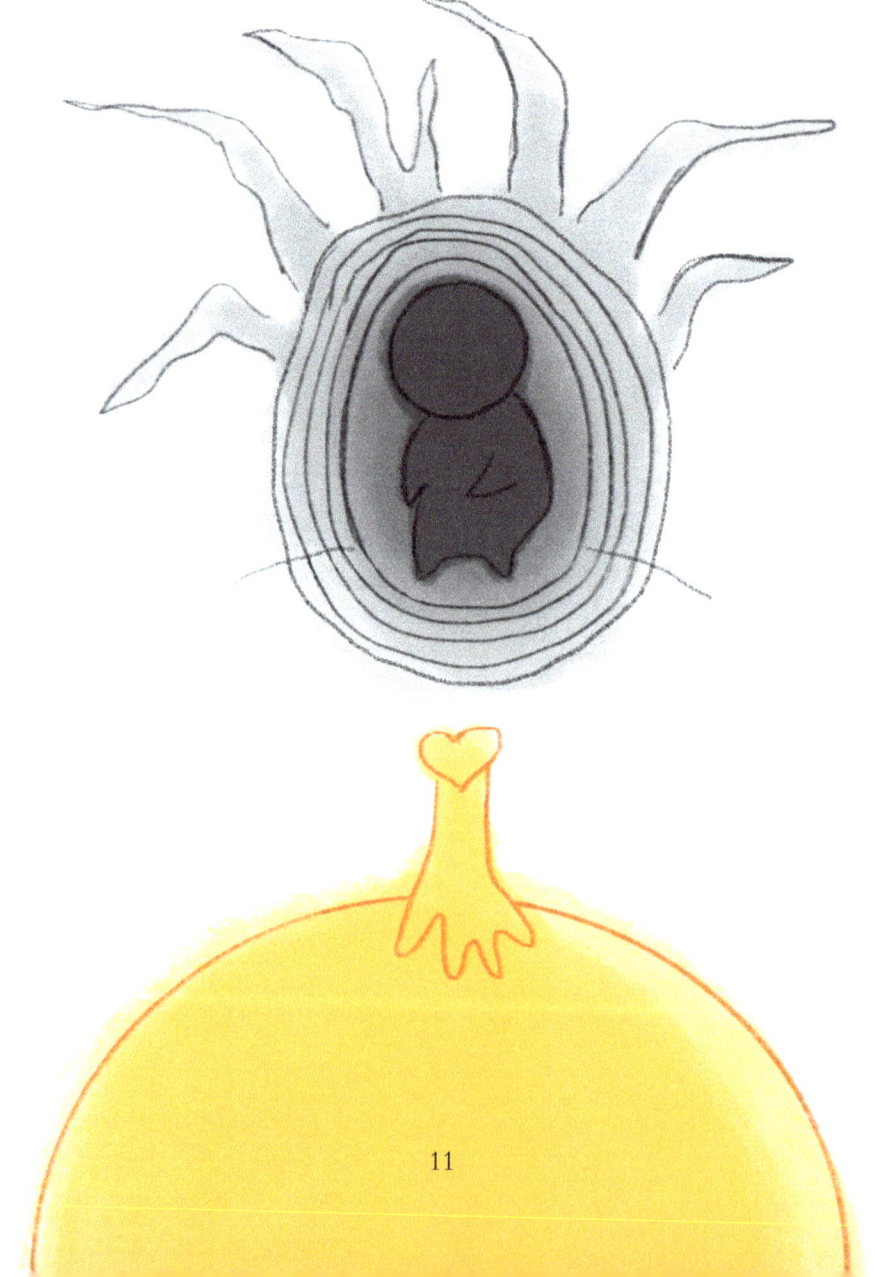

As our protective armour
grows heavy and thick,
we begin to lose sight of
our inner light.

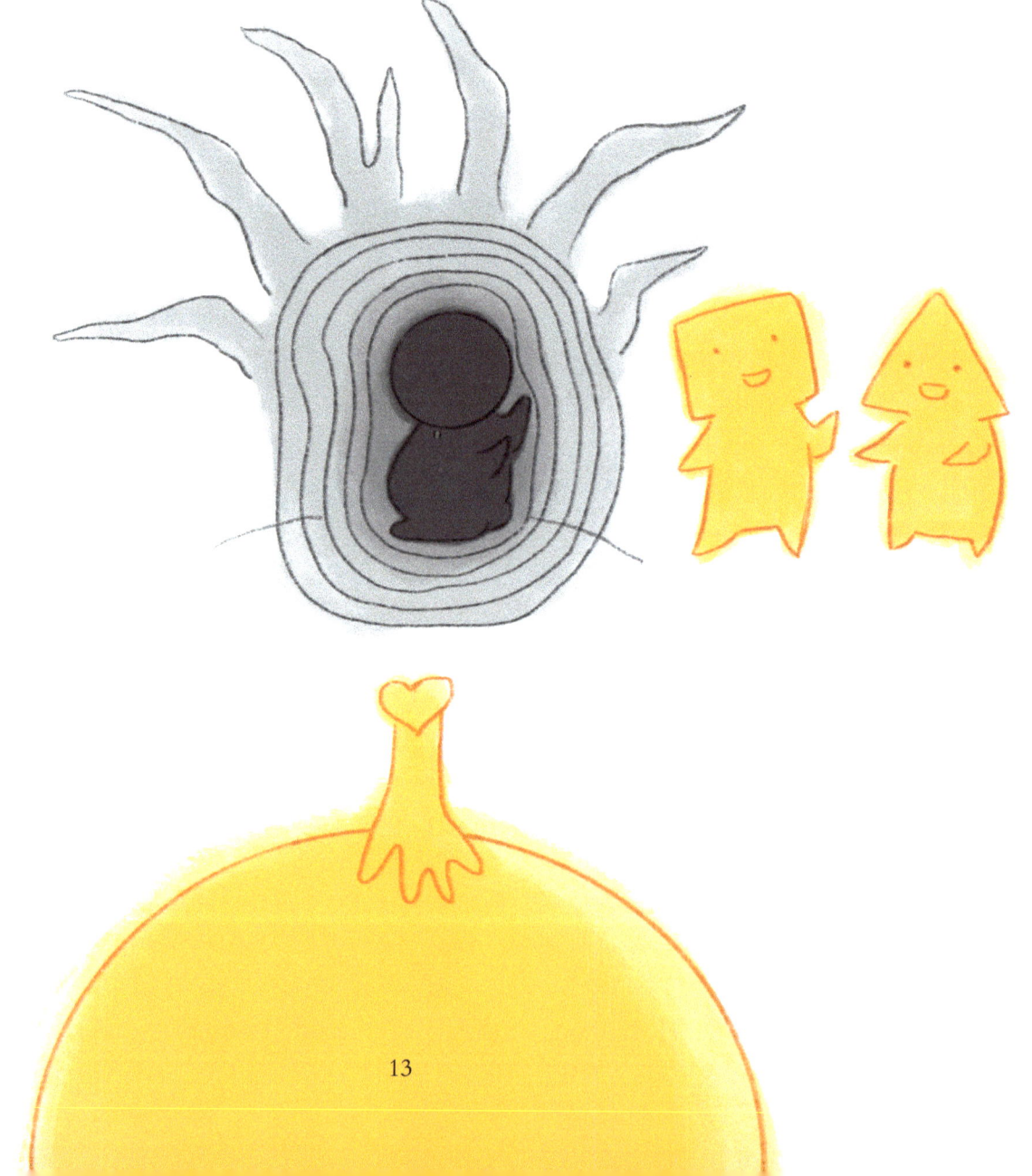

We survive the game of life,
yet we feel a disconnect,
a lack of fulfilment,
a yearning to be seen.

We look to anything that will
fill up the emptiness,
but the relief never lasts.

As the emptiness overtakes us,
we wonder how we can go on.

In these dark times,
we may hear a gentle, loving voice
call out from deep within…

*"This is not how things are meant to be.
A more radiant existence is possible."*

We follow the voice and
find a place of quiet stillness.

Away from the noise and distractions,
we finally hear what our Authentic Self
has been longing to say.

*"This is what brings me joy…
This is what is most important to me…
These are my unique gifts…
This is my true voice…"*

As we learn more about our Authentic Self,
we begin to fall in love with it.

We realize that our Authentic Self
has always been enough.
There is no more need for armour.

The protective layers fade away,
releasing our inner light.

Our roots can now grow deep
to nourish us with life energy
and hold us steady in every storm.

Our inner light expands,
transforming into branches
that are uniquely our own.

Abundant with loving energy,
we generously share it with others
who are also finding their way.

As more of us shed our layers
to reveal our inner truth,
we more easily see and celebrate
each other's unique way of being.

And as we do,
we eventually come to realize
the *radiant, beautiful whole*
that we all are.

REFLECTIONS

Guidance to support your journey.

Seeing the armour

Take some time to reflect on past experiences that have influenced your relationship with your Authentic Self:

- *As I was growing up, what lessons did I learn about the "right" and "wrong" ways of being?*

- *What kinds of armour did I create to protect my Authentic Self? How have they served me? How have they limited me?*

- *What kinds of armour might those close to me have worn? How might that have affected me?*

- *What is my current relationship with my Authentic Self?*

Reconnecting with your Authentic Self

In a quiet space, take a few minutes to breathe deep and connect with the sensations in your body. Imagine roots extending from your lower body and into the earth beneath, becoming a strong anchoring force. Visualize branches growing from your shoulders and arms, lifting your torso upwards.

As you embody this tree of radiant energy, gently feel into these questions:

- *What truly fills me up with joy? How might I invite more of this?*

- *What is most important to me? How might I prioritize this?*

- *What are my unique gifts? How might I offer more of this?*

- *What have I been longing to say or do? How might I express this?*

Daily practices

Similar to how daily exercise can improve your physical health, daily practices can strengthen your connection with your Authentic Self. Here are three simple activities you can try:

- **Write Morning Pages** - Each morning, fill up three pages of a notebook with stream-of-consciousness writing. Without judgement, allow all the voices in your head and heart to flow onto the page. *Learn more about this technique in the book "The Artist's Way" by Julia Cameron.*
- **Draw your energy tree** - Do the tree visualization exercise described on the previous page. Draw the image that comes up for you as you explore these questions: What does your energy tree look like right now? What nourishment do your roots need? What wants to grow from your branches?
- **Listen to your inner parts** - Take a few deep breaths and notice the physical sensations throughout your body. You may sense pain, stiffness, or movement in different areas. Choose one sensation to focus on. What does it feel like? Does it have an emotional quality? Without judgement, greet this inner part with a gentle "hello" and notice how it responds. You may try asking it some questions, such as: "What's behind the emotion that you're feeling? What would you like me to know?" Be curious and patient as you learn to listen to your inner parts. *Find out more about this powerful awareness technique in the book "The Power of Focusing: A Practical Guide to Self-Healing" by Anne Weiser Cornell, PhD.*

Finding a supportive community

Learning to express your Authentic Self can become an easier journey with the support of others. It's okay and sometimes necessary to ask for help. Take a moment to reflect:

> *What people in my life genuinely embrace my Authentic Self and encourage me to express it? How might I receive more support from them?*

Not everyone has a ready-made support network and that is absolutely alright. It may require proactive steps on your part to seek out or cultivate such a community. There are numerous avenues to explore, such as joining clubs or Meetup groups centered around shared interests, enrolling in classes, seeking guidance from a therapist or coach, or initiating a support group among friends.

Cultivating collective well-being

Consider ways that you can support the well-being of your family, friends, neighbours, and colleagues. Some examples:

- Check-in on them by occasionally asking: *"How are you doing, really?"*
- If they're in need of support, you can ask: *"How can I best help you? Would you like me to listen? Would you like me to help you problem-solve?"*
- Share what you appreciate about them and encourage them to express more of their Authentic Self: *"What fills you up with joy? What have you been longing to do? Let's think of ways we can do those things together."*

Take some time to reflect:

- *In what ways can I support the well-being of my family, friends, neighbours, and colleagues?*
- *Who is someone I'd like to check-in on right now?*

A message from the author

I hope you've enjoyed this story and found it helpful in some way. The images emerged in my journals as I tried to make sense of my own struggles and growth on the journey back to true Self. I am grateful for the support of many generous people who have helped me nurture my light and introduced me to diverse sources of wisdom. This story is inspired by several of these sources, including psychology, systems thinking, Confucianism, Taoism, Buddhism, Christianity, and Indigenous spiritual traditions. I've noticed a remarkable harmony among these ways of knowing, as if people throughout time, space, and culture have stumbled upon similar universal truths.

In our current landscape of pervasive mental health challenges, fragile social bonds, and unsustainable systems, these truths may hold even greater relevance. The path to well-being is not often apparent, and my hope is that this book can offer solace and gentle guidance to my fellow travellers. There is indeed a way to a more radiant individual and collective existence.

To the healers, guides, teachers, systems changemakers, and community cultivators, may this book serve as a nourishing resource as you care for others and yourselves.

With love,
Jessica

Acknowledgements

This book would not be possible without the generosity of my community. My heartfelt thanks go out to my incredible family, friends, mentors, and advisors. Your unwavering support, insightful teachings, thoughtful editing, and guidance throughout the publishing process have been invaluable. I'm also grateful to my many friends not named below who enthusiastically embraced the early drafts and gave input on the cover design. You have all been an important part of this journey!

Family:
Simon Fan and Hong Zuo
Aman, Jessie, Paul, Rav, and Sunny Sandhu

Friends, mentors, and advisors:
Adam Kahane (adamkahane.com)
Amanda Kwok (quietleader.co)
Amelia Zheng (ameliazheng.com)
Andres Marquez-Lara (Linkedin: andresmarquezlara)
Andres Ospina (@pinxelar)
Anthony L.
Ashley Good (failforward.org)
Avanti Garde
Benjamin Carr (lnkiy.in/pathwaystosource)
Bethany Deshpande
Bill Mei (billmei.net)
Brooking Gatewood
Chenny
Christie Wong (@mimaschrwonstie)
Crystal I. Zhou
Dasami Moodley
Eric Nehrlich (nehrlich.com/blog)
Estee Lee
Ha-Doan Le-Nguyen
Hans Krueger (hankrueg.com)
Jampa Alfieri (ZenRants.com)
Janet Quon
Jessica Leung
Josephine Pallandt
Josh To (@papiii.to)
Judy Gong
Kate Petriw
Katrina Bos (katrinabos.ca)
Liza Futerman (@human_thought_and_heartivism)
Markus Grupp
Martina Ng (BelightfulLiving.com)
Meghan Hellstern
Michelle Cochrane
Pamela W.
Peter Piasecki (visionplusbookkeeping.ca)
Quynh Nguyen
Roya Damabi
Sally Ng (thetripleeffect.com)
Sandy Jahmi Burg (www.learnfocusing.org)
Seishin
T. Lynn Stott
Teresa Hart (lnkiy.in/pathwaystosource)
Tim Sitt (freedomtomovegroup.com)
Toa M.
Victoria Chan (victoriakaychan.com)
Viola Hernandez (@fishydesign.studio)
Virabhadra Colin Bested
Yiannis Chrysostomidis (Linkedin: chrysostomidis)

Communities:
Conscious Asians (consciousasians.com)
River Delta Co-learning Community
ThinkBetter
Toronto Learning Nights
Willow Dharma House (growingwillow.org)
Tribe Network (tribenetwork.ca)
UFacilitate (ufacilitate.com)

About the author

Jessica Fan is deeply inspired by the question: "How can we cultivate resilient and thriving systems – within ourselves and with each other?" She explores this through her work as a holistic executive coach, systems change facilitator, design strategist, community cultivator, writer, artist, and musician.

Jessica resides in Toronto with her loving partner, family, and friends. She is known for her infatuation with round birds and her tendency to collect life stories of random strangers.

To learn more about Jessica's coaching, creative work, and free resources on finding Authentic Self, please visit: www.jessicafan.ca

AWAKING OCTOPUS PRESS

Awaking Octopus is a community platform dedicated to fostering our collective well-being. Through nourishing stories, new and ancient teachings, and spaces for deeper human connection, we create fertile ground for personal and systems transformation.

Stay updated on the latest community conversations and events through Instagram and Facebook: @awakingoctopus

www.ingramcontent.com/pod-product-compliance
Lightning Source LLC
Chambersburg PA
CBHW061127170426
43209CB00014B/1687